UN!CORN
FOOD

Magical Recipes for
Sweets, Eats & Treats

RACHEL
JOHNSON

STERLING EPICURE
New York

STERLING EPICURE
New York

An Imprint of Sterling Publishing Co., Inc.
1166 Avenue of the Americas
New York, NY 10036

ISBN 978-1-4549-3129-4

Distributed in Canada by Sterling Publishing Co., Inc.
C/o Canadian Manda Group, 664 Annette Street
Toronto M6S 2C8, Ontario, Canada
Distributed in the United Kingdom by GMC Distribution Services
Castle Place, 166 High Street, Lewes, East Sussex BN7 1XU, England
Distributed in Australia by NewSouth Books
45 Beach Street, Coogee, NSW 2034, Australia

For information about custom editions, special sales,
and premium and corporate purchases, please contact
Sterling Special Sales at 800-805-5489 or
specialsales@sterlingpublishing.com.

Manufactured in Canada

2 4 6 8 10 9 7 5 3

sterlingpublishing.com
Interior design by Christine Heun
Cover design by Elizabeth Mihaltse Lindy

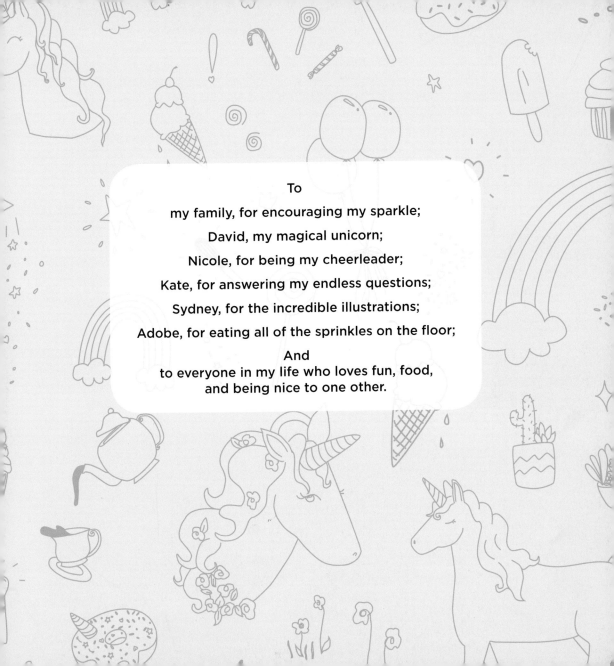

To

my family, for encouraging my sparkle;

David, my magical unicorn;

Nicole, for being my cheerleader;

Kate, for answering my endless questions;

Sydney, for the incredible illustrations;

Adobe, for eating all of the sprinkles on the floor;

And
to everyone in my life who loves fun, food,
and being nice to one other.

CONTENTS

SNACKS AND SWEETS

DRINKS

INTRODUCTION

Welcome to the wonderful world of *Unicorn Food*. Filled with plenty of sugar and magical recipes, this book is for those who seek joy in sprinkles, have glitter running through their veins, and believe that rainbows are a way of life. *Unicorn Food* will always give you joy, whether it's in making a recipe for your friends or decorating a birthday cake with sugar and fun. This book was written to create fun and fantasy in the kitchen by way of rainbows and unicorns.

With everything going on in the world, we need a reason to stop and celebrate little moments that give us joy. These moments of celebration *definitely* require sugar cookies brushed gold with edible luster dust. Or Choco-Tacos with homemade sprinkles. Or White Hot Chocolate—with glitter marshmallows. This book has *all* of that! Gather your pals and host a unicorn high tea or an impromptu rainbow party, *just because*.

The Internet has been a major inspiration for this book; rainbow-ifying everything from lattes to donuts has taken trending topics by storm, and these recipes deserve a permanent place on your shelf.

Whether you're looking to incorporate more edible glitter in your diet or need more tie-dye colored icing to reflect your lifestyle, all these recipes are Internet-approved and are definitely Instagrammable.

Let's just get this out of the way: no, unicorns are not real. But Swirly Sprinkle Celebration Cupcakes and Rainbow Sprinkle Waffle Cake and Eat-the-Rainbow Fruit Salad are very real and very delicious. The unicorn is the inspiration behind this entire cookbook in color, glitter, and uniqueness. Every recipe draws from the free and creative spirit of the unicorn, from Candy Mountain Creambows to the Real Deal Unicornchino (you know the one). It's up to you to channel your inner unicorn self and get in the kitchen!

Cheers to joy, happiness, and rainbow sprinkles!

UNICORN TOOL KIT

Pack your tool kit with everything you might need to become the ultimate unicorn foodicorn.

FOOD COLORING

There are three main groups of food coloring: gel, liquid, and natural. The multicolor packs you may find in the grocery store are most likely to be the liquid kind (in dropper bottles) and will do in a pinch. The best, most vibrant colors come from the highly concentrated gels found in most craft supply stores and easily available online. If you are looking for colors that are free of chemicals and additives, go for natural. Those colors are derived from highly pigmented foods such as beets, turmeric, and purple cabbage. Natural food colors are available in many specialty grocery stores and online. I like the India Tree® brand the best, but the three-color pack can be cost-prohibitive.

A note on dying batter: to make your life easier, dye batter in disposable paper bowls. Some of these recipes call for dividing batter and dying it in six different colors for rainbow layers, so give yourself a break and use paper to avoid the crazy cleanup.

PIPING BAGS/TIPS

Most large icing projects require a 16-inch bag, but you could get away with dividing icing into two 12-inch bags if that's all you have. It's better to get ahead of the game and use a large 16-inch bag instead of ending up with icing everywhere. I've also made the mistake of purchasing small packs of piping bags and individual bags, but they inevitably end up at the bottom of a bin for me to forget about promptly and repurchase the next time I need them. If you're a frequent sweets and treats maker, I recommend buying a restaurant-grade box of large bags to keep them organized and roll them out easily when needed.

When it comes to tips, I recommend trying out different shapes and patterns to get the look you love. There is no wrong answer when it comes to icing! My go-tos are an ⅛-inch and a ¼-inch plain and fluted tip, but I'll experiment with a star tip, mostly on cupcakes.

SPRINKLES

The world of pastry has moved past the rainbow jimmies! Mixing metallic dragées, colored rods, and a variety of colored spheres creates a unique dimension on otherwise plain sweets. See pages 92–93 for more on mixing the shapes, colors, and textures of sprinkles.

EDIBLE GLITTER/LUSTER DUST

If you're looking to coat your pastries in a gold finish, go for luster dust. Use a clear evaporating liquid as your medium (clear vanilla extract or vodka) and brush luster dust onto set fondant or solid candy coatings. If you're just looking for a sprinkling of glitter, go for edible disco dust. Hold the container a few inches above what you're trying to glitterfy and gently shake the container to coat evenly.

TOPPERS AND TOYS

Purchase cheap toys from the dollar store or online and spray paint them with metallic gold paint. Unicorn figurines, rainbows, shooting stars—plastic's the limit! Place painted toys on your treats as decoration or table accompaniments. Cut colored cardstock into shooting stars, rainbows, or sunburst shapes and tape them onto toothpicks or lollipop sticks for decoration.

CLEAR VANILLA EXTRACT

If you're looking to create bright white icing or transfer edible glitter or luster dust, be sure to seek out this specialty baking item. Now commonly found in the spices and extracts section of most grocery stores, this vanilla has a clarity that won't tint with a brown color like standard vanilla extract would. Also use clear vanilla as a medium to apply glitter or luster dust for décor.

OTHER SPECIAL ITEMS YOU MIGHT NEED

Mini muffin pan

Donut pan

Milkshake glasses

Stand mixer

Candy thermometer

BREAKFAST

Rainbow Swirl Bread
Unicorn Universe Baked Donuts
Vanilla Sprinkle Puff Cereal
Layered Rainbow Smoothies
Rainbow Pancake Stack
Rainbow Sprinkle Waffle Cake
Eat-the-Rainbow Fruit Salad

RAINBOW SWIRL BREAD

Every unicorn kitchen needs a staple bread recipe; this one just happens to be swirled with the colors of the rainbow! Let your imagination soar with this basic white bread recipe; think fairy toast, unicorn grilled cheese, and more.

MAKES 1 loaf bread
PREP TIME 2 hours
COOK TIME 1 hour

3 cups all-purpose flour

1 tablespoon granulated sugar

1 packet (¼ ounce) active dry yeast

1 cup whole milk at room temperature

1 large egg

2 tablespoons unsalted butter, softened

2 teaspoons kosher salt

Food coloring (red, orange, yellow, green, blue, purple)

1. In a large bowl or the bowl of a stand mixer, whisk together flour, sugar, and yeast. Add the milk, egg, butter, and salt and stir to combine.

2. If you are using a stand mixer, use the dough hook to knead the dough until it becomes smooth and elastic to the touch, about 5-8 minutes. If you don't have a stand mixer, stir the ingredients to combine and knead the dough on a clean floured surface and work it by hand until jt is smooth and elastic, about 10 minutes. Set the dough in an oiled bowl and cover it with a tea towel. Let it rise in a warm, dark place for at least 45 minutes or until it has doubled in size.

3. Punch the dough down and cut it into six even pieces. On a plastic cutting board (or any surface you're willing to dye with food coloring), add a different color of food coloring (about 4-5 drops or so) to each ball of dough and knead it until the color is fully incorporated. Use gloves to prevent your hands from staining; if you prefer, change the gloves between colors to prevent cross-contamination. After the color is consistent throughout the dough, place the balls of dough into six small separate bowls and cover to let rise another hour.

continued »→

4. One at a time, remove each colored ball of dough and gently roll it into an 8 × 4-inch rectangle about ½-inch thick. Stack the color rectangles on top of one another and roll the dough up into a log. Lightly grease a 9 × 5-inch loaf pan and set the dough into the pan. Let it rise another 45 minutes or until it has doubled in size.

5. Heat the oven to 375°F and bake the dough for 35 minutes or until it is lightly browned. Remove the loaf from the pan and let it cool completely on a rack.

UNICORN FOOD

CHEERS TO TOAST!

Tie-Dye Toast

In four small bowls, stir 2 tablespoons of cream cheese with 1 teaspoon of honey and 2 drops of food coloring (one bowl each of green, purple, and blue). Spread the toasted swirl bread with swirls of colored cream cheese and sprinkle with extra sprinkles and glitter.

Fairy Bread

Spread the toasted bread with the desired amount of softened butter and sprinkle with granulated sugar or colored sanding sugar and sprinkles.

UNICORN UNIVERSE BAKED DONUTS

When the galaxy glaze trend hit the Internet, bakers lost their minds creating swirled art on top of baked treats. Perfectly unperfect, the galaxy glaze technique intentionally streaks different colors of icing together, creating a canvas for shooting star sprinkles and glitter star dust.

MAKES about 24 small donuts
TOTAL TIME 45 minutes
YOU WILL NEED donut pan, large piping bag fitted with a ½-inch plain tip

FOR THE DONUTS

2½ cups all-purpose flour

1½ teaspoons baking powder

¼ teaspoon baking soda

¾ teaspoon salt

½ cup (1 stick) unsalted butter, softened

½ cup granulated sugar

⅓ cup brown sugar

2 large eggs

1 teaspoon vanilla extract

1 cup whole milk, warmed

FOR THE GLAZE

1¼ cups powdered sugar, sifted

1 tablespoon unsalted butter, melted

2 tablespoons heavy whipping cream

Food coloring (three colors of your choice)

Edible glitter, sprinkles (for garnish)

TO MAKE THE DONUTS

1. Preheat the oven to 425°F. Spray two six-count donut pans with nonstick cooking spray.

2. In a mixing bowl, sift together the flour, baking powder, baking soda, and salt. In a stand mixer (or a large bowl with hand mixer), beat together butter and sugars until smooth. Add the eggs and vanilla. Add the flour mixture and milk alternately and mix until just combined.

continued »→

TO MAKE THE DONUTS (*CONTINUED*)

3. To fill the donut pans, fill a large pastry bag (no tip required) with donut batter and pipe the batter into the wells of the pan, filling with about ¼ inch of room remaining. Or you can simply use a spoon to spread batter into the pan.

4. Bake the donuts for 10 minutes. Remove from the oven and wait a few minutes before turning them out of the pans onto a rack. Let them cool.

TO MAKE THE GLAZE

5. In a bowl, whisk together the sugar, melted butter, and heavy whipping cream. Divide the glaze into four bowls. Leave one bowl of glaze white and dye the other bowls of glaze to create a preferred color palette. By the spoonful, drop random scoops of glaze back into the main bowl. Use a knife to swirl the glaze gently.

TO DECORATE THE DONUTS

6. Dip each doughnut into the swirled glaze, placing it back on the cooling rack to set. Sprinkle with edible glitter and garnish with as many sprinkles as your unicorn heart desires.

7. The doughnuts will keep in an airtight container for up to 3 days.

VANILLA SPRINKLE PUFF CEREAL

Did you know you can *make* your own cereal? Sprinkle up
your breakfast bowl with this DIY crunch cereal!

MAKES 4 servings
PREP TIME 40 minutes
COOK TIME 30 minutes

1 ounce freeze-dried strawberries

1 cup all-purpose flour

¼ cup almond meal

½ teaspoon salt

1 large egg white

1 teaspoon vanilla extract

¼ cup brown sugar

1 tablespoon canola oil

2 tablespoons rainbow sprinkles

1 cup pink and blue mini marshmallows (if desired)

Milk of preference, to serve

1. Place the freeze-dried strawberries in a food processor or blender and crush them into a fine powder. If you'd rather, place the strawberries in a sealable storage bag and crush them with a rolling pin.

2. In the bowl of a stand mixer or a large bowl fitted with a hand mixer, combine the flour, almond meal, and salt. Add the egg white, vanilla, sugar, and oil and beat until the dough just comes together, adding sprinkles at the last moment. Turn the dough out onto a clean surface and form a ball.

3. Wrap the dough in plastic wrap and let it chill in the refrigerator for 20 minutes. Preheat the oven to 375°F and line a baking sheet with parchment.

4. Pinch the dough into small balls, about the size of a blueberry and bake until golden and set (about 12–15 minutes). You also can try shaping the dough into stars or hearts.

5. Let the donuts cool completely. Serve with cold milk and marshmallows, if desired. Store in an airtight container for up to 1 week.

LAYERED RAINBOW SMOOTHIES

Smoothies in multiple colors are as enticing as the rainbow looks—sip on the magic of natural fruit smoothies that are layered to create a rainbow of goodness. Make one smoothie in one color and pour the mixture evenly into six glasses; simply clean out the blender with a quick rinse and repeat the process with the remaining smoothie colors. Keep it simple by dividing the recipe in half and going for a three-color palette such as pink, blue, and purple or yellow, green, and pink.

MAKES 6 smoothies (about 2 servings of smoothie for each color)
PREP TIME 20 minutes
YOU WILL NEED blender

RED/PINK SMOOTHIE	YELLOW SMOOTHIE	ORANGE SMOOTHIE	GREEN SMOOTHIE	BLUE/PURPLE SMOOTHIE
½ cup strawberry Greek yogurt	½ cup plain Greek yogurt	½ cup plain Greek yogurt	½ cup plain Greek yogurt	½ cup plain Greek yogurt
½ cup nonfat milk	½ cup nonfat milk	½ cup orange juice	½ cup green juice	½ cup grape juice
½ cup frozen cherries	1 frozen banana	1 frozen banana	1 frozen banana	1 frozen banana
1 cup frozen strawberries	1 cup frozen pineapple chunks	1 cup frozen mango chunks	1 cup packed fresh spinach	1 cup frozen berries
1 handful ice cubes	1 handful ice cubes	1 handful ice cubes	1 cup frozen pineapple chunks	1 handful ice cubes
			1 handful ice cubes	

> Add all the ingredients to a blender and blend until smooth.

MORE
SMOOTHIE IDEAS

Rainbow Smoothie Popsicles

Instead of glasses, pour the smoothies into 12 Popsicle®
molds and freeze overnight or for at least 6 hours. To pack
the protein, add a pinch of chia seeds or raw oats to the
bottom of the molds for a complete breakfast.

Rainbow Smoothie Bowls

Swirl layers of a smoothie into a bowl format and
garnish with toppings such as shredded unsweetened
coconut, chia seeds, balls of dragon fruit (or other
colorful fruits), star fruit cutouts, and crumbled granola.

RAINBOW PANCAKE STACK

Stack the rainbow, piled high! These light and fluffy pancakes are dyed in rainbow hues and topped with decadent maple whipped cream. Share this pile of pancakes with friends by slicing the stack like a cake!

SERVES 4
PREP TIME 15 minutes
COOK TIME 30 minutes

2½ cups all-purpose flour

2 tablespoons sugar

½ teaspoon salt

¼ teaspoon baking soda

2 large eggs

1½ cups buttermilk or nonfat plain yogurt

2 tablespoons unsalted butter, melted and cooled

Rainbow food coloring (red, orange, green, etc.)

Nonstick cooking spray

1 cup heavy whipping cream

2 tablespoons maple syrup, plus more for serving

1. In a large bowl, whisk together the flour, sugar, salt, and baking soda. In another bowl, whisk together the eggs, buttermilk (or yogurt), and melted butter. Add the egg mixture to the flour mixture and whisk until just combined. Let the pancake batter sit for 10 minutes. Divide the batter into six bowls (opt for paper for easy cleanup) and and gently stir in 5–6 drops of food coloring: one bowl for red, one for orange, and so on, to complete the rainbow.

2. Heat a griddle or nonstick pan over medium-high heat and spray it with nonstick cooking spray. Add one color of batter onto the pan (this will make one large pancake) and cook the pancake until bubbles have risen to the surface and the edges firm up (about 3 minutes). Flip the pancake and cook until golden brown, about 3–5 minutes, and set the pancake on a plate. Repeat the process with the other colored batter colors to make 6 pancakes. Keep the pancakes in a warm oven until ready to serve.

3. In a large bowl, vigorously whip heavy cream until soft peaks form, about 5 minutes. Gently fold in the maple syrup.

4. Remove the pancakes from the oven and stack them one colored pancake on top of another in a rainbow pattern. Top with desired amounts of maple whipped cream and extra syrup.

RAINBOW SPRINKLE WAFFLE CAKE

You don't need to settle for a basic breakfast—up your brunch game with this stacked waffle cake piled high with fresh fruit and colorful waffle layers. Stack this "cake" on a stand for the ultimate birthday breakfast, complete with heaps of rainbow sprinkles and fun!

MAKES 4-6 servings
PREP TIME 45 minutes
YOU WILL NEED waffle iron, cake stand, baking rack

FOR THE WAFFLES

- 1 cup all-purpose flour
- 1 tablespoon sugar
- 1 teaspoon baking powder
- ½ teaspoon salt
- 1 cup whole milk, at room temperature
- 2 large eggs, lightly beaten
- 4 tablespoons unsalted butter, melted
- Nonstick cooking spray

FOR THE FILLING

- ¾ cup sugar
- 8 ounces cream cheese, softened to room temperature
- ½ cup vanilla Greek yogurt
- 8 ounces fresh strawberries, tops removed and sliced
- 8 ounces fresh blueberries
- 1 tablespoon honey
- Whipped cream (for topping)
- Rainbow sprinkles (for garnish)

TO MAKE THE WAFFLES

1. Preheat a waffle iron (if your iron indicates how dark the waffles can get, set it on a medium-to-light setting).

2. Combine the flour, sugar, baking powder, and salt in a large bowl and make a well in the middle of the dry ingredients. Add the milk, eggs, and butter and whisk until smooth. Let sit for 10 minutes or until the batter is starting to bubble and rise.

3. Spray the waffle iron with nonstick cooking spray and fill with one cup of batter. Close the top and bake until the waffle is lightly golden brown. Remove the waffle from the waffle iron, and let it cool completely on a baking rack. Repeat with the remaining batter to makes four waffles.

TO MAKE THE FILLING

4. While the waffles are cooling, make the filling. In the bowl of a stand mixer or a bowl fitted with a hand mixer, cream the sugar and cream cheese until light and fluffy. Fold in the Greek yogurt and fill a piping bag (with the desired tip) with frosting.

5. In a small bowl, toss the strawberries and blueberries in the honey. Let the mixture sit for 10 minutes or until it is macerated and juicy.

TO ASSEMBLE THE CAKE

6. Swipe a small amount of frosting on the plate or cake stand on which you are assembling the cake. Set one waffle on the plate and fill with a layer of icing and fruit. Repeat with the remaining waffles and top with a silly amount of whipped cream and sprinkles. Cut like a cake and serve!

EAT-THE-RAINBOW FRUIT SALAD

Treat your body like the temple it is and feed it fruits of every color in the rainbow! Bright, fresh tropical fruits are tossed in a honey syrup and fresh mint for a breezy spin on this salad. Use whatever fruit happens to be in season instead of the ones listed in the ingredients. Be sure to use as many colors as you can to create a rainbow effect.

MAKES 4-6 servings
TOTAL TIME 20 minutes

1 cup dragon fruit balls or cubes

1 cup papaya balls or cubes

1 cup cantaloupe balls or cubes

1 cup pineapple balls or cubes

1 cup diced cucumber

1 cup purple grapes

2 tablespoons honey

2 tablespoons warm water

½ teaspoon kosher salt

5 mint leaves, chopped (if desired)

1. Separate the fruit into small bowls, one for each fruit.

2. In another bowl, whisk together the honey and water until the honey is dissolved.

3. To the honey/water mixture, add salt and mint (if desired).

4. Divide the seasoned honey/water mixture among the small bowls of fruit, adding an equal amount to each bowl.

5. Toss each bowl of fruit.

6. On a large serving platter, arrange the fruits in a striped rainbow pattern as shown in the photo.

REAL FOOD

Tie-Dye Grilled Cheese
Super Healthy Unicorn Soups
Ombre Tomato Toast
Rainbow Rolls
Rainbow Veggie Bowls
Savory Rainbow Crepes
DIY Rainbow Pasta
Rainbow Vegetable Kebabs
Unicorn Tea Party
Rainbow Crudités with Unicorn Dip

TIE-DYE GRILLED CHEESE

Don't freak out, but this is the grilled cheese of your dreams.
The multicolored cheese pull is just perfect
to generate a "like" for your Instagram˙!

MAKES 2 sandwiches
PREP TIME 15 minutes

4 ounces shredded
mozzarella

4 ounces shredded Cheddar

4 ounces shredded Gruyère

Food coloring (pink,
green, blue, and purple),
8 drops each, divided use

4 tablespoons softened
butter

8 (½-inch) slices white
bread (such as sourdough,
pullman, or brioche)

Kosher salt, to taste

Edible glitter (optional)

1. Mix the cheeses together
in a large bowl. Divide between
4 bowls and tint each cheese
with each food coloring by
stirring around with a spoon
(about 2 drops per color per
bowl will do).

2. Heat a nonstick pan or
griddle to medium-high heat.
Spread the butter evenly on one
side of each bread slice.

3. Place four slices of bread,
butter side down, on the heat
surface. Top with each color of
cheese in any preferred pattern.
Sandwich with another slice of
bread, butter side up. Cook on the
griddle for 2–3 minutes or until the
cheese is starting to melt. Flip and
cook another 2 minutes, or until
the bread is toasty and golden.

4. Sprinkle with salt and edible
glitter in case you are Extra. Enjoy
the sandwich after dipping into
Super Healthy Unicorn Soups
(page 33)!

SUPER HEALTHY UNICORN SOUPS

Some recipes are so easy to make that it seems magical. These soups have different ingredients, but all follow the same set of instructions. If you don't like a certain color of vegetable, simply substitute another similarly colored vegetable. No matter which one you choose, these soups are supremely simple and delicious!

EACH SOUP MAKES 6–8 servings
PREP TIME 30 minutes

RED SOUP

- 2 tablespoons olive oil
- 2 cloves garlic, minced
- 1 white onion, chopped
- 1 pound red beets, peeled and chopped
- 1 can (14.5 ounces) low-sodium vegetable stock
- 2 teaspoons kosher salt
- ½ teaspoon cracked black pepper
- 1 tablespoon fresh lemon juice

ORANGE SOUP

- 2 tablespoons olive oil
- 2 cloves garlic, minced
- 1 white onion, chopped
- 1 pound chopped butternut squash
- 1 can (14.5 ounces) low-sodium vegetable stock
- 2 teaspoons kosher salt
- ½ teaspoon cracked black pepper
- 1 tablespoon fresh lemon juice

YELLOW SOUP

- 2 tablespoons olive oil
- 2 cloves garlic, minced
- 1 white onion, chopped
- ½ pound cauliflower florets
- ½ pound parsnips, peeled and chopped
- 1 can (14.5 ounces) low-sodium vegetable stock
- 2 teaspoons kosher salt
- ½ teaspoon cracked black pepper
- 1 tablespoon fresh lemon juice

continued ▶▶

GREEN
SOUP

2 tablespoons olive oil

2 cloves garlic, minced

1 white onion, chopped

2 cups fresh spinach

1 large Yukon Gold potato, chopped into rough pieces

1 can (14.5 ounces) low-sodium vegetable stock

2 teaspoons kosher salt

½ teaspoon cracked black pepper

1 tablespoon fresh lemon juice

PURPLE
SOUP

2 tablespoons olive oil

2 cloves garlic, minced

1 white onion, chopped

1 pound purple potatoes, peeled

½ pound purple cauliflower

1 can (14.5 ounces) low-sodium vegetable stock

2 teaspoons kosher salt

½ teaspoon cracked black pepper

1 tablespoon fresh lemon juice

TO MAKE ALL THE SOUPS

1. In a large Dutch oven or pot, heat the olive oil over medium-high heat. Add the garlic and onion and cook until softened (about 5–7 minutes).

2. Add the vegetables, broth, and just enough water to cover the vegetables. Bring to a boil and reduce heat to low, simmering until the vegetables are tender, about 15–20 minutes.

3. Working in batches, puree the soup in a blender at high speed until smooth, allowing some steam to escape by removing the cap from the blender and covering the opening with a thick dish towel.

4. Alternatively, use an immersion stick blender to blend directly in the pot. Add more water to achieve the desired consistency.

5. Season with salt, pepper, and lemon juice to taste.

OMBRE TOMATO TOAST

Top your toast with herbed ricotta cheese and top-of-the-season tomatoes, perfect for showing off the colors of summer. A delicious tomato can be a hard-to-find unicorn in the off-season; opt for greenhouse-grown tomatoes for the best flavor any time of year.

MAKES 10 toasts
PREP TIME 15 minutes

1 pound mixed multicolored tomatoes (yellow or green heirloom, purple kumato, red cherry)

1 tablespoon plus 1 teaspoon kosher salt

1 cup fresh ricotta cheese

Zest of 1 lemon

2 tablespoons finely chopped basil leaves

1 tablespoon finely chopped chives

1 baguette French bread, cut in ½-inch-thick slices on the diagonal (8–10 slices)

2 tablespoons extra virgin olive oil

1 whole garlic clove

Flaky sea salt and cracked black pepper, to taste

1. Preheat the oven to broil. Slice the tomatoes and toss with 1 tablespoon of salt in a large bowl and let sit for 10 minutes.

2. In a small bowl, fold the ricotta, lemon zest, basil, chives, and remaining salt.

3. Brush the bread slices with olive oil and place on a baking sheet. Place the bread slices on the lowest oven rack and toast under the broiler, flipping after 2 minutes, and toast until browned. Transfer the bread to a plate and let it cool slightly. Rub the raw garlic clove on the edges of the bread pieces and sprinkle with flaky sea salt.

4. Smear the ricotta evenly on the bread. Top with the tomatoes and garnish with flaky salt and cracked black pepper.

RAINBOW ROLLS

Celebrate colorful veggies by wrapping them in a transparent rice wrapper, making them perfect for dipping. This dish is great for a dinner party or gathering with friends—get your guests to help you roll!

MAKES 10 rolls
PREP TIME 30 minutes

8 ounces rice vermicelli noodles

10 (8-inch) rice spring roll papers

1 medium beet, peeled and thinly sliced

1 yellow bell pepper, sliced into thin strips

1 large carrot, shaved into thin ribbons

1 ripe mango, peeled and sliced into thin strips

1 thinly sliced jalapeño, if desired

3 sprigs fresh mint leaves

1 bunch fresh cilantro

Sweet chili sauce or peanut sauce for dipping

1. Bring a small pot of water to a boil and cook the noodles for 5 minutes (or until soft) and drain. Set aside to cool.

2. Set up your spring roll station. Fill a shallow dish with hot water and set aside. Prepare all the vegetable ingredients, organize on a plate, and clear a cutting board for rolling.

3. One at a time, dip rice paper in water for 10–15 seconds and shake gently to remove excess water. Lay the paper flat on a cutting board. In a horizontal row across the center of the wrapper, arrange the veggies in a rainbow pattern (optional jalapeño), about 2 inches uncovered on each side. Top with mint and cilantro leaves.

4. Fold the uncovered sides inward over the filling and tightly roll the wrapper up from the bottom (like wrapping a burrito). Press the wrapper gently to secure and set aside on a serving platter and cover with a damp paper towel to keep moist. Repeat with the remaining rolls.

5. When all rolls are prepared, remove paper towel and arrange the rolls in a circular pattern around the dipping sauce. Garnish with any extra herbs, and enjoy!

RAINBOW VEGGIE BOWLS

Glam up your lunch with these grain bowls. Don't be afraid to get creative with your toppings. Use cookie cutters to cut radish or beet slices into star shapes

MAKES 2 servings
PREP TIME 25 minutes

FOR THE VEGGIES

- ½ cup grain of choice (such as quinoa or farro), cooked to package directions
- 1 cup chopped kale
- 2 tablespoons olive oil
- 2 teaspoons kosher salt
- 1 small candy stripe or golden beet, peeled and thinly sliced
- 1 watermelon radish, thinly sliced
- ½ yellow bell pepper, sliced into strips
- 1 large carrot, peeled and shaved into ribbons
- ½ small avocado, peeled and thinly sliced
- ¼ cup diced cucumber

Optional: edible flowers, microgreens

FOR THE DRESSING

- ½ cup Greek yogurt
- ¼ cup fresh Italian parsley leaves, finely chopped
- 2 tablespoons water
- 1 peeled garlic clove

Zest of 1 lemon

- 2 tablespoons fresh lemon juice
- 1 tablespoon extra virgin olive oil
- ¼ teaspoon salt
- 1 tablespoon sesame seeds or preferred spice blend

1. Let the grains cool and set aside. In a bowl, massage kale, olive oil, and 1 teaspoon salt with your hands.

2. The kale should be soft and reduced by half in volume.

3. Sprinkle the vegetables with the remaining salt. Divide the grains into two bowls and top with vegetables and edible flowers in a pretty pattern that shows off all the colorful veggies!

4. For the dressing, blend Greek yogurt, parsley, water, garlic, lemon zest, lemon juice, olive oil, and salt in a blender until smooth. Drizzle onto grain bowls and sprinkle with sesame seeds or other preferred spice blend.

SAVORY RAINBOW CREPES

Crepes don't always have to be sweet. Fill these colorful crepes with fillings such as ham and cheese or smoked salmon to give a salty flavor to these superthin pancakes.

MAKES about 10 crepes
PREP TIME 40 minutes
COOK TIME 20 minutes

1 cup all-purpose flour

1 tablespoon granulated sugar

¼ teaspoon kosher salt

1½ cups whole milk, at room temperature

4 large eggs

3 tablespoons unsalted butter, melted and cooled

Food coloring (3 colors of your choice)

Desired fillings (see "Crepe Filling Ideas" on page 41)

1. In a blender, combine the flour, sugar, salt, milk, eggs, and butter. Blend on high speed until the mixture is smooth, about 30 seconds. Let the batter rest for at least 30 minutes. Divide the batter into three bowls and dye each bowl with 4–5 drops of one food coloring, stirring to distribute the color.

2. Heat a 10-inch nonstick pan, or a crepe pan if you own one, over medium-low heat and brush with butter. Working quickly, add 2 tablespoons of each batter to the pan and swirl to cover the bottom of the skillet completely. Adding a bit of each batter to the pan will create a swirled, tie-dye effect. Cook until the underside of the crepe is lightly golden brown, about 3 minutes. Flip and cook another minute, or until the crepe is just set. Transfer to a plate and top with a layer of waxed paper to separate from the other crepes while they are cooling.

3. Repeat with the remaining batter, coating the pan with butter as needed. Fill the crepes with the desired fillings (see the sidebar) by adding toppings to the top half of each crepe. Fold horizontally and then again vertically for an easy-to-eat triangle. Enjoy immediately!

CREPE FILLING IDEAS

Black Forest Ham, Dijon Mustard & Swiss

Spread the top half of the crepes with a thin layer of good-quality Dijon mustard. Top with two slices of ham and two slices of cheese.

Cream Cheese, Smoked Salmon & Dill

Spread the crepe with a thin layer of cream cheese and sprinkle with fresh dill leaves. Top with 1 ounce of smoked salmon slices.

Wilted Spinach & Gruyère

Warm 1 tablespoon of olive oil in a skillet over medium-high heat. Add 1 clove of garlic (minced) and stir until fragrant. Add a handful of spinach and stir to wilt, cooking until the liquid evaporates. Sprinkle the crepe with shredded Gruyère and top with wilted spinach.

Almond Butter & Strawberry Preserves

Spread the crepe with a thin layer of almond butter and top with preserves.

Sliced Tomatoes & Prosciutto

Top the crepe with thinly sliced tomatoes and sprinkle with kosher salt. Garnish with 2 slices of prosciutto.

DIY
RAINBOW PASTA

Use natural food dyes to give this pasta a variety of colors, and shape it into fun bow-tie shapes. It's a perfect project for a girls' night in or a colorful dinner date!

MAKES 1 pound pasta
PREP TIME 1 hour
COOK TIME 90 seconds
YOU WILL NEED pasta maker or rolling pin, fluted pasta roller (optional)

3 cups all-purpose flour

1½ teaspoons kosher salt

6 large eggs, at room temperature

3 teaspoons extra virgin olive oil

All-natural food coloring (4 colors of your choice)

Semolina flour, for dusting

Sauce of your choice, such as Marinara or simple melted butter or cheese, warmed

1. In a mixing bowl, whisk together the flour and salt and make a well in the flour mixture. Crack the eggs into the well and whisk with a fork, gradually whisking in the flour until the dough just comes together.

2. Turn the dough out onto a clean floured surface. Knead the dough a few times and add the olive oil one teaspoon at a time, kneading after each addition, until the dough is smooth and elastic. Form a ball and cover it in plastic wrap. Let it rest at room temperature for at least 30 minutes.

3. Divide the dough into four pieces. Using gloves to protect your hands, smear 3–4 drops of one food color onto the top of one piece of dough. On a surface protected with a sheet of plastic, knead the color

into the dough until smooth. Set that piece aside, and repeat with the remaining dough pieces.

4. Using a pasta machine or rolling pin, roll the pasta into thin rectangular sheets to about ⅛-inch thickness. Dust each sheet with semolina and cut the pasta into 1½ x 1 inch pieces. Use a fluted pasta cutter to decorate the edges. Along the long side, pinch each rectangle in the middle firmly to make a bow-tie shape. (Alternatively, cut sheets into thin strips for noodles and dust with more semolina to keep separate.)

5. Drop the pasta into rapidly boiling water and cook it for 90 seconds, using a long-handled strainer to drain. Toss in a sauce of your choice and enjoy!

UNICORN FOOD

RAINBOW VEGETABLE KEBABS

Stack the rainbow onto grillable skewers and perfect
your summertime gathering! Drizzle with zesty, bright green
chimichurri dressing after grilling to impress your guests.

MAKES 8 skewers
PREP TIME 20 minutes
COOK TIME 20 minutes
YOU WILL NEED 8 wooden skewers, grill pan or grill

FOR THE SKEWERS

16 cherry tomatoes

1 orange bell pepper, cored
   and cut into 1-inch squares

1 yellow squash, cut into
   ½-inch-thick slices

1 yellow bell pepper, cored
   and cut into 1-inch squares

1 zucchini, cut into ½-inch-
   thick slices

1 green bell pepper, cored
   and cut into 1-inch squares

1 large red onion, peeled,
   quartered, and cut into
   bite-size pieces

   Nonstick cooking spray

1 teaspoon kosher salt

FOR THE CHIMICHURRI DRESSING

¼ cup extra virgin olive oil

1 tablespoon chopped
   Italian parsley

1 tablespoon chopped fresh
   cilantro

2 tablespoons red wine
   vinegar

1 clove garlic, minced

½ teaspoon kosher salt

¼ teaspoon freshly cracked
   black pepper

1. Set the skewers in a shallow
dish and cover with water. Let
the skewers soak for at least
20 minutes, which will prevent
them from burning on the grill.

2. Thread the vegetables evenly onto the skewers in a rainbow pattern: red (tomatoes), orange (bell pepper), yellow (yellow squash and bell pepper), green (zucchini), and blue/purple (red onion). Spray the skewers with nonstick cooking spray and sprinkle with salt to season.

3. Prepare the grill or set a grill pan over medium-high heat for use indoors. Spray the grill or pan with nonstick cooking spray.

4. In a mini food processor or blender, add olive oil, parsley, cilantro, vinegar, garlic, salt, and pepper, and process on high speed until smooth and emulsified. Set aside until ready for use.

5. Cook the kebabs 5–7 minutes on each side or until grill marks appear and the vegetables are soft. Set the skewered kebabs on a serving platter and drizzle with herb dressing to serve.

UNICORN TEA PARTY

It's always a proper afternoon for unicorn high tea! Gather your gals for tea time, complete with snacks and treats fit for a unicorn queen. Serve your favorite kind of tea at the party in the prettiest pot you can find.

SPRINKLE SCONES

MAKES: 8 SCONES

- 1 cup powdered sugar, sifted
- 2 tablespoons whole milk
- Pink food coloring
- 8 mini vanilla bean scones (store-bought)
- Sprinkles and colored sugar

1. In a bowl, mix together the powdered sugar, milk, and pink food coloring until smooth. Set the scones on a cooling rack and drizzle with glaze. Sprinkle with the desired amount of sprinkles and sugar. Let the icing set for 30 minutes or until hardened.

RAINBOW TEA SANDWICHES

MAKES: 12 SANDWICHES

- 6 slices rainbow swirl bread (see page 13 for recipe)
- 1 cup deli salad of choice (such as egg or chicken)

1. Spread three slices of bread evenly with salad, all the way to the edges. Press the remaining bread slices on top to make three complete sandwiches. Cut into four triangles.

PRISM PINWHEELS

MAKES: ABOUT 10 PINWHEELS

- 4 slices white bread, crusts removed
- 1 cup whipped cream cheese
- 2 tablespoons granulated sugar
- 1 teaspoon vanilla extract
- Food coloring (purple, pink, green)
- 2 tablespoon rainbow sprinkles

1. Set a sheet of plastic wrap flat on a clean surface. Lay the bread slices in a horizontal line with a slight overlap. Cover with another piece of plastic wrap and flatten the bread into one long rectangle

COMPLETE THE MENU

Pastel petit fours

Rainbow Sprinkle Cream Puffs
(see page 74 or recipe)

Macaroons

with a rolling pin. In a small bowl, stir the cream cheese, sugar, and vanilla until smooth. Divide into three bowls and dye with food coloring, stirring to incorporate. Remove the top layer of plastic and spread the pinwheels with cream cheese colors in three horizontal sections. Starting from the bottom, roll the bread tightly to create one long log. Wrap in the bottom layer of plastic and refrigerate for 20 minutes. Cut the log into 1-inch slices, garnish with sprinkles, and serve.

RAINBOW CRUDITÉS WITH UNICORN DIP

Crudités is a fancy word for "vegetables for dipping." When dippable veggies in a variety of colors are paired with an herby dip, it makes a delicious rainbow combo dish that is a snacker's delight. Don't skimp on the herbs in the dip; it gets its bright-green color from all the fresh herbs it contains.

MAKES about 1½ cups dip
PREP TIME 20 minutes
CHILL TIME 45 minutes

FOR THE CRUDITÉS

Assorted snackable vegetables in a variety of colors (select many different colored ones to get a rainbow effect)

FOR THE DIP

2 cups packed baby spinach

½ cup packed fresh basil leaves

2 tablespoons chopped fresh chives (plus more for garnish)

1 tablespoon chopped fresh tarragon

Zest of 1 lemon

⅓ cup mayonnaise

½ cup plus 1 tablespoon full-fat Greek yogurt, divided use

¼ cup fresh lemon juice

1 whole garlic clove

TO MAKE THE CRUDITÉS

1. Cut the veggies into bite-size pieces and arrange in a rainbow pattern on a platter around the Unicorn Dip (see the photo on the facing page).

TO MAKE THE DIP

2. Combine the spinach, basil, chives, tarragon, and lemon zest in a food processor and pulse until finely chopped. Add the mayonnaise, ½ cup Greek yogurt, lemon juice, and garlic and blend until smooth.

3. Pour the dip into a serving bowl and swirl with the remaining Greek yogurt. Decorate with chives and serve with crudités.

SNACKS
AND SWEETS

Unicorn Movie Mix
Unicorn Layer Cake
Unicorn Fruit Roll-Up
Rainbow Crepe Cake
Swirly Sprinkle Celebration Cupcakes
Sprinkle Cake Truffles
Watermelon Layer Cake with Colorful Fruits
Rainbow Shaved Ice
Rainbow Sherbet Choco-Tacos
Rainbow Sprinkle Cream Puffs
Candy Mountain Creambows
Glitter Pink Strawberry Marshmallows
Magic Meringue Pops
Strawberry Cereal Stacks
Fantastic Funnel Cakes
Magically No-Fail Sugar Cookies

UNICORN MOVIE MIX

Put on your favorite movie and munch on this unicorn movie mix.
The popcorn is coated in pink-and-blue chocolate and tossed with
candy-coated pretzels, sprinkles, and more delicious things!

MAKES about 6 cups
PREP TIME 30 minutes
CHILL TIME 1 hour

1 (3.2-ounce) bag popped popcorn (lightly salted flavor)

1 cup white chocolate candy melts

3 teaspoons canola oil, divided use

1 cup butter snap pretzels (about 20 pretzels)

Food coloring (blue, pink, and purple), 9 drops each, divided use

Disco glitter and sprinkles

½ cup pastel chocolate-coated candies

20 frosted animal cookies

1 cup dehydrated strawberries

1. Line two baking sheets with parchment paper and fill one sheet with a layer of popcorn.

2. Transfer the candy melts to a microwave-safe bowl and heat for 30 seconds at a time, stirring after each interval until smooth. Divide into three bowls and stir 1 teaspoon of canola oil and 3 drops of each food color to each bowl.

3. Dip the pretzels into the colored chocolate, shaking to remove excess chocolate, and set onto the remaining baking sheet. Drizzle the popcorn with the remaining melted chocolate in any preferred pattern. Garnish the popcorn and pretzels with sprinkles and glitter, and let set, about 1 hour.

4. In a large bowl, toss the popcorn, pretzels, candies, animal cookies, and strawberries. Store in an airtight container up to 1 week. Enjoy!

UNICORN LAYER CAKE

Are you ready for a challenge? Building a unicorn cake is a somewhat time-consuming process, but you've got this. You are a magical baker unicorn, and you need to wow your friends with this rainbow cake. Channel your creativity and transform a white layer cake into the prettiest unicorn your cake stand has ever seen! Serve the cake in slices and watch the smiles appear!

SERVES 8–10
ACTIVE TIME 2 hours
COOLING TIME 2 hours
YOU WILL NEED kitchen scale, 8-inch round cake pans (at least two),
2 large heavy-duty pastry bags fitted with a large tip of your choice,
offset spatula (for smoothing frosting) or bench scraper,
cake stand (at least 10 inches in diameter)

FOR THE CAKE

2½ cups all-purpose flour

1½ cups granulated sugar

1 teaspoon baking soda

1 teaspoon baking powder

1 teaspoon salt

1 cup canola oil

¾ cup full-fat plain yogurt (not Greek)

¾ cup water

4 large egg whites

2 teaspoons vanilla extract

Food coloring (red, orange, yellow, green, blue, purple), about 4–5 drops of each color for each cake layer

1 cup simple syrup (see "Super Simple Syrup" on page 60)

FOR THE FROSTING

3 sticks unsalted butter, at room temperature

4 cups powdered sugar

2 tablespoons whole milk

½ teaspoon kosher salt

continued »→

FOR THE UNICORN EFFECTS

1 ice cream cone

2 ounces fondant, divided use

3 ounces white chocolate

Optional, as needed for decoration: sour candy belts, store-bought macaroons mini star cookies, glitter, sprinkles, edible star candies

TO MAKE THE CAKE

1. Preheat the oven to 350°F. Prepare 8-inch round cake pans by lightly greasing them with butter or cooking spray and dusting with flour, knocking the pans to remove the excess flour. For an extra measure, insert a round of parchment paper to ensure that the layers come out of the pan cleanly.

2. In a large bowl, whisk together the flour, sugar, baking soda, baking powder, and salt. Make a well in the middle of the flour mixture and add the oil, yogurt, water, egg whites, and vanilla extract. Stir the batter until the batter is smooth. Be careful not to overmix.

3. Using a kitchen scale, weigh the batter. Divide the batter into six equal-sized portions and distribute into six bowls. To each bowl, add 4–5 drops of one food coloring and stir gently with a spoon to fully incorporate the color.

4. Working with however many cake pans you have, fill the pans with one batter color and shake to distribute the batter to the edges. Knock the bottom of the pan against the counter to send any remaining air bubbles to the top. Bake the cake layers for 10–12 minutes, or until the tops are slightly browned. Brush with a thin layer of simple syrup and transfer to a cooling rack and let cool completely. Wash the pans in cool water and repeat the process with the remaining color layers.

TO MAKE THE FROSTING

5. Combine the butter and 2 cups of powdered sugar in a stand mixer and mix on low until smooth. Add the remaining powdered sugar, milk, and salt, and gradually increase the speed until the frosting is fluffy, about 5 minutes. If the frosting is too stiff, add 1 tablespoon milk until the desired consistency is reached.

6. Fill two large pastry bags (fitted with a large tip) with icing and keep one bag of icing in the fridge until ready to use.

TO ASSEMBLE AND FROST THE CAKE

7. Line the edges of the cake stand with small strips of parchment paper to protect the surface from icing. Add a small amount of frosting to the middle of a cake stand and begin layering the cake in a rainbow pattern, starting with the purple cake and stacking in a rainbow pattern up to red cake. These layers should be fairly flat, as a small amount of batter was used, but if the layers seem too round on the tops, shave some cake off the layer using a long serrated knife or cake leveler. Rounded layers will make this cake difficult to stack.

8. Spread one layer of the cake with roughly ⅓ inch of frosting and repeat with the remaining cake layers. Press the top of the cake gently to secure it. (It's okay if some frosting comes out on the sides.)

9. Cover the whole cake with a thin layer of frosting, creating a crumb coat layering. Don't worry about the cake looking perfect at this point; that's what the other frosting bag is for.

10. Let the cake chill in the fridge for at least 1 hour. Clean your work surface and set up your decorating station.

11. When the cake has chilled, take it out of the fridge and cover it with the remaining frosting. Use an offset spatula or dough scraper to smooth out the frosting. Run the spatula or scraper under hot water to clean off excess frosting buildup.

12. Let the cake chill another hour in the fridge. Carefully slide out parchment liners to expose the outer rim of the cake stand, and clean off any excess frosting.

TO CREATE THE UNICORN EFFECTS

13. To create the horn, cover a standard ice cream cone with fondant or white chocolate and varnish it with gold luster dust. Alternatively, build a horn with fondant by spiraling one rope of fondant with a wooden skewer to hold it in place. If fondant isn't your friend, you can cut out a unicorn horn–shaped cookie (see page 89 for Magically No-Fail Sugar Cookies) and varnish with gold luster dust.

14. Create fondant teardrop shapes for ears and for eyes. Let the fondant dry out for a few hours before placing it onto the cake to avoid drooping.

15. For the mane, swirl colored frosting (see page 65 for swirling tips) or place twirled sour candy belts to create beautiful locks.

16. For extra effects, decorate your cake to the max with store-bought macaroons and mini star cookies and go crazy with glitter, sprinkles, and edible star candies. Decorate the cake to your unicorn heart's true desires! Use the photo on page 56 as a guide to positioning the unicorn parts.

SUPER SIMPLE SYRUP

One of my favorite tricks for perfect layers of cake is a brush of simple syrup after the layers come out of the oven. The sugary syrup locks in moisture and protects the tops during the icing process.

Combine equal parts of water and sugar in a small saucepan and simmer until the sugar has dissolved.

Alternatively, combine equal parts of water and sugar in a microwave-safe bowl and microwave in 1-minute intervals, stirring until the sugar has dissolved completely.

UNICORN FRUIT ROLL-UP

Every lunch box deserves a sweet snack made with delicious and beautiful fruits! You don't need the store-bought roll-ups—making these treats is super easy. Feel free to switch up the fruits for your favorite flavors.

MAKES about 6 fruit strips
PREP TIME 20 minutes
COOK TIME 3 hours
YOU WILL NEED food processor or blender. standard size kitchen twine, rimmed baking sheet

- 4 ounces strawberries, trimmed
- 3 tablespoons fresh lemon juice, divided use
- 4 ounces blueberries
- 1 cup fresh mango, chopped

1. Preheat the oven to the lowest setting, preferably 180°F.

2. Line a rimmed baking sheet with parchment paper.

3. In a food processor or blender, purée the strawberries with 1 teaspoon lemon juice until smooth. Pour the purée onto the baking sheet in a horizontal line and spread into a thin layer (about ⅛ inch).

4. Rinse the food processor or blender, and repeat with the blueberries. Repeat again with the mango. When spreading the fruit purées onto the baking sheet, slightly overlap them to create one large rectangle.

5. Place the baking sheet in the oven until completely dry and no stickiness remains, about 3 hours.

6. Cut the fruit leather into strips (with the parchment paper) and roll up, securing with kitchen twine or tape. Store in an airtight container at room temperature for up to 1 week.

RAINBOW CREPE CAKE

If you're looking for a no-bake version of a rainbow layer cake, look no farther than this crepe cake. Stacked high with thin layers of rainbow-colored crepes, it js filled with rich pastry cream to make a light and delightful dessert.

SERVES 8–10
PREP TIME 1 hour
CHILL TIME 5 hours

FOR THE CREAM FILLING

- 2¼ cups whole milk, divided use
- 6 large egg yolks, at room temperature
- ⅔ cup granulated sugar, divided use
- ⅓ cup cornstarch, sifted
- 2 teaspoons vanilla extract

FOR THE CREPES

- 1 cup all-purpose flour
- 1 tablespoon granulated sugar
- ¼ teaspoon kosher salt
- 1½ cups whole milk, at room temperature

- 4 large eggs, at room temperature
- 3 tablespoons unsalted butter, melted and cooled
- Food coloring (red, orange, yellow, green, blue, purple)

FOR TOPPING

- 1 cup whipped cream
- Sprinkles and glitter, to garnish

TO MAKE THE CREAM FILLING

1. In a medium-size bowl, whisk together ½ cup milk, egg yolks, ⅓ cup sugar, and cornstarch. Transfer the remaining milk to a saucepan and add the vanilla extract. Add the remaining sugar and bring to a soft simmer over medium heat, whisking occasionally.

2. Take the saucepan off direct heat and carefully and gradually whisk the egg mixture into the milk. Return the pan to heat and cook, whisking constantly until the mixture thickens (about 2 minutes).

3. Remove from heat and transfer to a bowl. Press plastic wrap directly onto the surface of the cream and chill until cold, about 4 hours (you can do this a day ahead).

TO MAKE THE CREPES

4. In a blender, combine the flour, sugar, salt, milk, eggs, and butter. Blend until the mixture is smooth, about 30 seconds. Let the batter rest for at least 30 minutes. Divide the batter into six bowls and dye with food colors, stirring to distribute the color.

5. Heat a 10-inch nonstick pan over medium-low heat and brush with butter. Add 2 tablespoons of each batter into the pan and swirl to completely cover the bottom of the skillet. Cook until the underside of the crepe is lightly golden brown, about 3 minutes. Flip and cook another minute or until the crepe is just set. Transfer to a plate and separate with layers of waxed paper. Repeat with the remaining batter, coating the pan with butter as needed.

TO ASSEMBLE THE CAKE

6. Swipe a small amount of pastry cream onto the surface of a cake stand at least 12 inches in diameter. Add one crepe and spread with 3 tablespoons of pastry cream. Repeat with the remaining crepes and cream. Let chill for at least 1 hour. Top the cake with whipped cream and sprinkles. Enjoy!

SWIRLY SPRINKLE CELEBRATION CUPCAKES

This cupcake puts the *fun* in *funfetti*! Go for the extra glitter and sprinkles with these cupcakes to celebrate any occasion. Did you pass a big test? More glitter! Maybe you got a promotion? Extra sprinkles! Did you get up in the morning and have a good day? Blow out the candles. Even the smallest moments are worth celebrating.

MAKES 36 cupcakes
PREP TIME 40 minutes   BAKE TIME 20 minutes
YOU WILL NEED food coloring, sprinkles, celebration candles, 3 small pastry bags,
1 large heavy-duty pastry bag, ¼-inch pastry tip (preferred shape)

FOR THE CUPCAKES

2½ cups all-purpose flour

1½ cups granulated sugar

1 teaspoon baking soda

1 teaspoon baking powder

1 teaspoon salt

1 cup vegetable or canola oil

¾ cup full-fat plain yogurt (not Greek)

¾ cup water

4 large egg whites

2 teaspoons vanilla extract

Food coloring (blue, purple, and pink, or three colors of your choice)

FOR THE FROSTING

3 sticks unsalted butter, at room temperature

4 cups powdered sugar

1 teaspoon vanilla extract

½ teaspoon kosher salt

Food coloring (blue, purple, and pink, or three colors of your choice)

Optional, as needed for decoration: sprinkles, disco glitter

TO MAKE THE CUPCAKES

1. Preheat the oven to 350°F. Prepare two 12-count cupcake tins with liners.

2. In a large bowl, whisk together the flour, sugar, baking soda, baking powder, and salt. Make a well in the middle of the flour mixture and add the oil, yogurt, water, egg whites, and vanilla. Stir the batter until the egg whites are well incorporated and the batter is smooth; be careful not to overmix.

3. Divide the batter evenly into three bowls and add 2–3 drops of food coloring to each. Mix the batter gently to incorporate the color fully. Scoop 1 heaping tablespoon of each

color batter into each cup and swirl the batter with a toothpick or clean butter knife.

4. Bake the cupcakes for 20 minutes or until the tops are lightly browned. Let rest for 2 minutes and transfer to a cooling rack to let cool completely.

TO MAKE THE FROSTING

5. Combine the butter and 2 cups of powdered sugar in a stand mixer and mix on low until smooth. Add the remaining powdered sugar, vanilla, and salt and gradually bring up the speed until the frosting is fluffy, about 5 minutes. Divide the icing into three bowls and add 2–3 drops of food coloring to dye to your shades of blue, purple, and pink, or other colors of your preference. Fill three pastry bags with each icing color. Fit the large pastry bag with a tip. Snip the tips of the three colored icing bags and fit them into the large bag (this will create the swirled effect). Squeeze the top to push the icing colors down to the icing tip and practice the swirls by piping out some icing onto a paper towel. Once the icing is properly swirled, frost each cupcake and decorate it to your unicorn heart's desire.

6. Decorate the cupcakes with sprinkles, candles, and disco glitter to your heart's content!

SPRINKLE CAKE TRUFFLES

Let's get real, cake balls are a crock of nonsense. You know the ones with the perfectly spherical balls of cake, suspended on lollipop sticks and covered in chocolate? They take approximately one hundred years to make and I've had about 10 percent success rate when I've attempted them. These cake truffles can come from any leftover cake (even a box mix!) and come together in a pinch. Nobody will miss the sticks!

MAKES 40 cake balls
PREP TIME 1 hour
BAKE TIME 30 minutes
YOU WILL NEED cookie scoop, cooling rack (2)

2½ cups all-purpose flour

1½ cups sugar

1 teaspoon baking soda

1 teaspoon baking powder

1 teaspoon salt

1 cup vegetable or canola oil

¾ cup full-fat plain yogurt (not Greek)

¾ cup water

4 large eggs

2 teaspoons vanilla extract

Food coloring, in 3 different colors of your choice

3 (16-ounce) containers store-bought vanilla frosting, divided use

¼ cup decorating sprinkles

1. Preheat the oven to 350°F. Coat a 13 × 9-inch baking dish with nonstick cooking spray.

2. In a large bowl, whisk together flour, sugar, baking soda, baking powder, and salt. Make a well in the middle of the flour mixture and add oil, yogurt, water, eggs, and vanilla. Stir the batter until the eggs are well incorporated and the batter is smooth. Be careful not to overmix.

3. Divide the batter evenly into three separate bowls and add 5–6 drops of food coloring into each bowl. Mix the batter gently to fully incorporate color.

4. Distribute the batter into the baking dish, one scoopful at a time to create a tie-dye pattern. Smooth out the batter and carefully lift the dish a few inches into the air, dropping the dish onto the counter to knock out any air bubbles.

5. Bake the cake for 25–30 minutes, or until the top is browned. Let it cool completely on a cooling rack (this can be done a day ahead).

6. When the cake is cool, crumble it by the fistful into a large bowl until the cake becomes small, even crumbs. Break up any large pieces with your fingers. Add 3 cups of frosting to the cake and stir to create an even filling.

7. Using a cookie scoop (the squeeze-and-release type works best), pack the cake into the scoop as best as you can, turning the cake balls out onto the cooling racks. Repeat with the remaining cake. Let chill 15 minutes.

8. In a microwave-safe bowl, heat the remaining icing in 30-second increments until it has a thin, pourable consistency. Set the cooling racks with the cake balls onto foil-lined baking sheets (for easier cleanup) and pour icing over the cake balls; cover completely. Decorate the cake balls with sprinkles and let them set another 15 minutes in the fridge before serving.

WATERMELON LAYER CAKE WITH COLORFUL FRUITS

The "healthiest" sweet in the book, this "layer cake" is made from slabs of watermelon and garnished with star-shaped fruit cutouts. For a dairy-free and vegan version, skip the Greek yogurt in the filling.

SERVES 8–10
PREP TIME 25 minutes
YOU WILL NEED 1 wooden skewer, small star-shaped cookie cutters

1 medium-size watermelon

1 large Granny Smith apple, cored and cut into ¼-inch slices

2 tablespoons freshly squeezed lemon juice

1 large honeycrisp apple, cored and cut into ¼-inch slices

10 large strawberries, washed and trimmed

½ cup vanilla bean Greek yogurt

9 ounces frozen whipped coconut topping, thawed

1 teaspoon vanilla extract

1 pint fresh blueberries

2 tablespoons shredded unsweetened coconut

1. Using a sharp knife and a secure cutting board, cut off the top and bottom of the watermelon to create a flat surface and set the watermelon upright. Carefully cut off the rind by running a knife in a curved pattern alongside the watermelon. Discard the rind. Cut the watermelon into 1-inch-thick slices and let it sit on a paper-towel–lined baking sheet.

2. Using the cookie cutters, cut star shapes out of the Granny Smith apple and brush with lemon juice to preserve the color. Discard (or snack on!) excess apple. Brush honeycrisp apple slices with lemon juice and set aside. Slice half of the strawberries into ¼-inch slices (this doesn't have to be perfect) and set aside, leaving half of the strawberries whole.

3. In a small bowl, combine the Greek yogurt, whipped coconut topping, and vanilla extract until smooth.

4. Assemble the cake. Stack one layer of watermelon onto a cake stand and begin lining the edge of the surface with honeycrisp apple slices, blueberries, and some apple stars (leaving at least a few for the top), allowing some slices of the fruit to peek out of the sides. Fill the center with 1 cup of cream filling and repeat with the remaining layers.

5. Secure the cake by placing a wooden skewer in the middle (be sure to measure how tall the cake is and cut the skewer accordingly). To complete the cake, top it with whole strawberries and any remaining fruit. Sprinkle with coconut to complete the cake. Slice and serve immediately.

RAINBOW SHAVED ICE

Granita is a fancy word for "shaved ice" made right in a standard freezer. Vibrant fruits are transformed into these light and icy desserts, making for a rainbow of sweet treats!

MAKES about 3 cups granita
PREP TIME 15 minutes
CHILL TIME 2 hours 45 minutes

RED
ICE

- ¾ cup granulated sugar
- 1 cup hot water
- 2 tablespoons lemon juice
- 10 ounces frozen strawberries

YELLOW
ICE

- ¾ cup granulated sugar
- 1 cup hot water
- 2 tablespoons lime juice
- 10 ounces frozen pineapple chunks

BLUE
ICE

- ¾ cup granulated sugar
- 1 cup hot water
- 2 tablespoons lime juice
- 10 ounces frozen blueberries

ORANGE
ICE

- ¾ cup granulated sugar
- 1 cup hot water
- 2 tablespoons lime juice
- 10 ounces frozen passion fruit puree

GREEN
ICE

- ¾ cup granulated sugar
- 1 cup hot water
- 2 tablespoons lime juice
- 1 cantaloupe, peeled and cubed (seeds removed)

PURPLE
ICE

- ¾ cup granulated sugar
- 1 cup hot water
- 2 tablespoons lemon juice
- 10 ounces frozen cherries

UNICORN FOOD

MORE GRANITA IDEAS

Make it boozy

Serve granitas with a splash
of Prosecco or Cava.

Creamy granita

Serve granita shards over a
scoop of ice cream or topped
with sweetened condensed milk.

TO MAKE ALL THE ICES

1. Pour the sugar, hot water, and lime or lemon juice into a blender and blend to dissolve.

2. Add the fruit and blend until smooth.

3. Pour the mixture into a 9 × 9-inch baking dish and place in the freezer, uncovered, for 45 minutes.

4. Remove from the freezer and scrape the icy mixture with a fork. Cover with aluminum foil and let freeze another 2 hours.

5. Remove from the freezer and scrape the frozen mixture with the teeth of a fork until a slush mixture forms.

6. Scoop into short glasses and serve with a spoon

RAINBOW SHERBET CHOCO-TACOS

Next to the ice cream sandwich, the choco-taco is arguably the freezer's best ice cream novelty offering. These unicorn-inspired treats are filled with rainbow sherbet and dipped in decadent white chocolate. This recipe does require a waffle cone maker, but ask around on Facebook to see if a friend will let you borrow one.

MAKES 18 choco-tacos
PREP TIME 45 minutes
CHILL TIME 2 hours

FOR THE TACO SHELLS

- 2 large eggs plus 2 large egg whites, at room temperature
- 1 teaspoon kosher salt
- 1 teaspoon vanilla extract
- ¼ cup plus 1 tablespoon light brown sugar
- 1 cup all-purpose flour
- 4 tablespoons unsalted butter, melted
- 2 tablespoons whole milk

FOR THE FILLING AND TOPPING

- 12 ounces rainbow sherbet
- 6 ounces white chocolate candy coating disks
- 2 tablespoons coconut oil
- Sprinkles, for decorating

TO MAKE THE SHELLS

1. Whisk together the eggs, egg whites, salt, vanilla extract, and sugar. Mix in the flour until just combined. Pour in butter and milk and whisk until smooth. Preheat the waffle cone maker and grease with nonstick cooking spray. While the maker is preheating, wrap a small book with a 1-inch spine with plastic wrap and set up a wire cooling rack to rest the shells. Drop 1 tablespoon of batter onto the center of the maker and close to cook, about 1–2 minutes. Protecting your hands with two layers of paper towels,

immediately remove the waffle disk from the maker and carefully shape it into a taco by bending it over the spine of the book. Hold for a minute to secure and let the shell cool completely on the wire rack. Repeat with the remaining batter.

TO ASSEMBLE THE
CHOCO-TACOS

2. Assemble the choco tacos. Line a baking sheet or dish (that will fit in your freezer) with parchment. Remove the sherbet from the fridge and allow it to soften slightly for 8–10 minutes. Using a teaspoon or small cookie scoop, spoon the sherbet into the shells and transfer it to the baking sheet. Repeat with the remaining sherbet and shells and freeze the tacos for about 30 minutes.

3. Melt the chocolate in a microwave-safe bowl in 30-second intervals, stirring in between, until smooth (about 90 seconds). Stir in the coconut oil and dip the tops of the choco-tacos into the chocolate, immediately decorating it with sprinkles and transferring it back to the freezer to refreeze for another 15 minutes or until ready to serve.

RAINBOW SPRINKLE CREAM PUFFS

Turn up the fun with these baked pastry puffs, pipe with rainbow sprinkle pastry cream, and top with more decor. Serve at your Unicorn Tea Party (see page 46), a baby shower, or another colorful occasion.

MAKES about 20 puffs
PREP TIME 1 hour 30 minutes   COOK TIME 1 hour
YOU WILL NEED 1 large pastry bag fitted with a ½-inch plain tip, 1 large pastry bag fitted with a ¼-inch tip

FOR THE PUFFS

- ½ cup (1 stick) unsalted butter, cut into pieces
- 1 teaspoon sugar (optional)
- ½ teaspoon salt
- 1 cup all-purpose flour
- 5 large eggs, at room temperature, divided use
- 6 ounces white chocolate candy coating discs
- Rainbow sprinkles of choice, for decoration

FOR THE CREAM FILLING

- 2 cups cold, heavy whipping cream
- ⅓ cup powdered sugar
- 2 tablespoons rainbow nonpareil sprinkles

TO MAKE THE PUFFS

1. Preheat the oven to 375 degrees. In a medium saucepan over medium-high heat, combine butter, sugar, salt, and 1 cup water. Bring to a boil and quickly stir in the flour with a wooden spoon. Continue to stir until a film forms on the bottom of the pan. Remove from heat and transfer dough to a bowl to cool slightly, about 3 minutes. Add 4 eggs to the dough, one at a time, stirring vigorously to entirely incorporate the egg after each addition. Transfer the dough to a large pastry bag, fitted with a ½-inch tip.

2. Line a baking sheet with parchment paper and pipe 1½-inch rounds of dough onto the prepared pans, about 2 inches apart. Make an egg wash by whisking together the remaining egg and 1 tablespoon water. Dip your finger in water and gently smooth the tops (having rounded tops will ensure even baking). Brush with the egg wash and bake until the puffs are golden brown, about 30 minutes. Let the puffs cool completely on a wire rack.

TO MAKE THE CREAM FILLING

3. In a stand mixer or bowl fitted with a hand mixer, whip the whipping cream for about 3 minutes, or until stiff. Fold in the powdered sugar and sprinkles.

4. Transfer the cream to a pastry bag fitted with a ⅛-inch plain round tip. Insert the tip into the bottom of each pastry, and pipe to fill with about 2 tablespoons of filling.

TO FINISH

5. Place white chocolate discs in a microwave-safe bowl. Microwave in 30-second intervals, stirring after each interval until the white chocolate is smooth, about 90 seconds. Top each pastry with a drizzle of white chocolate and garnish with sprinkles. Serve within 24 hours.

CANDY MOUNTAIN CREAMBOWS

Take a trip up to Candy Mountain! These marshmallow-topped cookies, piled high with cream filling and decorated with edible glitter , will be the star of any unicorn-themed gathering. This recipe was inspired by the Krembo, a traditional Israeli treat topped with marshmallow filling and covered in chocolate.

MAKES 12 creambow cookies
PREP TIME 45 minutes active time   COOLING TIME 5 hours
YOU WILL NEED candy thermometer, piping bag

11 ounces white chocolate candy coating discs

12 golden sandwich cookies

1 cup sugar

⅓ cup water

4 egg whites

Pinch of cream of tartar

Food coloring (three colors- pink, blue, and purple)

Optional: Edible stars and/or glitter

1. Set a cooking rack into an aluminum-foil lined baking sheet. Place white chocolate discs in a microwave-safe bowl. Microwave in 30-second intervals, stirring after each interval until chocolate is smooth, about 90 seconds. Using a fork, gently dip cookies into the white chocolate, tapping to remove excess. Set cookies on cooling rack and let harden.

2. Place the sugar and water in a small saucepan and dissolve over low heat. Simmer until a candy thermometer reads 235°F. If you don't have a candy thermometer, you can drop a small bit of the heated sugar into a bowl of ice water. If the mixture holds together, the sugar is ready.

continued »→

3. While the sugar is heating up, whip the egg whites with an electric mixer on high speed until foamy. Add the cream of tartar and continue whipping at medium speed. Once the sugar syrup is ready, carefully drizzle it into the mixing bowl while the mixer is running. Keep whipping the whites until the mixture is stiff and glossy, about 5 minutes. Spoon the marshmallow filling into a pastry bag fitted with a ½-inch round tip.

4. Fold over the long sides of the pastry bag (fitted with the tip) and paint vertical lines of food coloring onto the inside of the bag. Spoon marshmallow filling into the bag.

5. Line a baking sheet with parchment paper and fit with a cooling rack. Place the cookies on the rack, about 1 inch apart. Carefully pipe a 3-inch mountain of cream filling onto each cookie and finishing with a peak at the top. Sprinkle with edible stars or glitter, if desired.

6. Let the cookies set on the counter for at least an hour. They will keep in an airtight container in the fridge for at least a week.

GLITTER PINK STRAWBERRY MARSHMALLOWS

MAKES about 12 large marshmallows
PREP TIME 30 minutes   COOLING TIME 8 hours
YOU WILL NEED candy thermometer, handled mesh sifter

1½ cups water, divided use

4 (1-ounce) envelopes powdered gelatin

3 cups granulated sugar

1¼ cups light corn syrup

½ teaspoon kosher salt

½ teaspoon strawberry flavor extract

5–6 drops pink food coloring

2 tablespoons unsweetened flaked coconut

¼ cup mixed sprinkles

2 tablespoons powdered sugar

2 tablespoons cornstarch

Edible glitter, for garnish (if desired)

1. Coat a 9 × 9-inch baking dish with nonstick cooking spray. Line with a square of parchment paper and spray again with nonstick spray.

2. Pour ¾ cup water into a stand mixer bowl fitted with a whisk attachment, and sprinkle gelatin on top.

3. Set a small saucepan with the remaining water, sugar, corn syrup, and salt over medium heat. Cook until the sugar dissolves and stir once. Cook another 12–15 minutes without stirring or until the temperature reaches 210°F. Set aside to cool slightly.

4. With the mixer on low, pour the sugar mixture slowly into the gelatin mixture. Gradually increase the speed to high and beat until thick and fluffy and triple in volume, about 8–10 minutes.

5. Spray a spatula with nonstick cooking spray. Working quickly, stir the strawberry extract, and pink food coloring and gently fold to incorporate the color fully. If you prefer to keep the color swirled, stop after a few folds. Pour the marshmallow mixture into the coated dish, smooth the top, and garnish with sprinkles.

6. Set the marshmallows aside in a cool place (do not keep in the fridge; the moisture will ruin them).

7. Combine the powdered sugar and cornstarch in a small bowl and dust the top of the marshmallows, using a mesh strainer or a sifter with a handle. Carefully turn the marshmallows onto a clean cutting board lightly dusted with powdered sugar. Coat a sharp knife with nonstick cooking spray and cut the marshmallows into 12 even squares. Toss in the remaining powdered sugar mixture and garnish with edible glitter, if desired. The marshmallows will keep in an airtight container for up to 5 days.

MAGIC MERINGUE POPS

Looking for a fabulously gluten-free treat idea? These easy meringue pops are perfect for those with allergen sensitivities. If you're missing the lollipop sticks, simply pipe meringue batter into flat discs or little kisses. These shapes also work for decorating the Unicorn Cake or other treats!

MAKES about 12 pops
PREP TIME 20 minutes
COOK TIME 1 hour
YOU WILL NEED large pastry bag fitted with ⅝-inch fluted tip, large lollipop sticks

4   large egg whites, at room temperature

½   teaspoon cream of tartar

1   cup granulated sugar

Food coloring (three colors of your choice)

Rainbow sprinkles of your choice

1. Prepare the pans. Line two baking sheets with parchment paper. Draw circles about 2½ inches in diameter onto the parchment paper and stage a lollipop stick about 1½ inches into the center of the circle. Alternate placement of the circles to fit about 6 pops on each sheet.

2. Preheat the oven to 200°F. In a stand mixer, beat the egg whites and cream of tartar at medium speed until frothy. Pour the sugar slowly into the bowl and beat until the sugar is dissolved and stiff peaks form.

3. Add drops of the food coloring onto the sides of the pastry bag in a random pattern. Spoon the meringue into the pastry bag and set in a tall drinking glass. Pipe the meringue into circles on top of the pops, swirling the food coloring as you go.

4. Top with sprinkles and bake for 45 minutes or until the meringues are set and stiff. Let cool on the sheets for at least 30 minutes.

STRAWBERRY CEREAL STACKS

Everybody loves a crispy rice treat! Add some magic by sprinkling in dehydrated strawberries crushed into a fine powder with a blender or food processor. Your treats will take on a naturally pink hue and berry flavor, ideal for a white chocolate drizzle and extra sprinkles!

MAKES 12 treats
PREP TIME 20 minutes
COOLING TIME 2 hours

¼ cup dehydrated strawberries

½ cup (1 stick) unsalted butter

12 ounces mini marshmallows

½ teaspoon kosher salt

4 cups puffed rice cereal

4 cups berry-flavored cereal

½ cup white chocolate candy coating disks

Sprinkles and edible glitter, for decoration

1. Grease an 8 × 8-inch baking dish with nonstick cooking spray. Set a large stockpot over medium-high heat.

2. In a blender or food processor, pulse the strawberries into a fine powder.

3. Melt the butter and marshmallows and stir until smooth. Stir in the salt and strawberry powder. Add the cereal and toss until well coated.

4. Pour the cereal mixture into the baking dish. With buttered hands or a cooking spray–coated spatula, press the cereal mixture into the pan to create an even surface. Let cool for 2 hours.

5. Turn the pan over onto a cutting board and cut the treats into 12 even pieces. Melt the candy disks in a small bowl in the microwave in 30-second intervals, stirring in between, until smooth. Drizzle onto treats in any desired pattern and sprinkle with the desired amount of sprinkles and glitter.

6. Let set for 15 minutes and enjoy! The treats will keep in an airtight container for up to 2 weeks.

FANTASTIC FUNNEL CAKES

You don't need to head to the circus to enjoy a funnel cake! Funfetti cake batter is deep fried at home into a nest of crunchy, puffy dough. Dusted with rainbow sprinkles and powdered sugar, of course! Traditionally, funnel cake uses an actual funnel to swirl the batter, but a pastry bag is the safer option with this batter.

MAKES 8 funnel cakes
PREP TIME 20 minutes   COOK TIME 30 minutes
YOU WILL NEED frying thermometer, large pastry bag fitted with a ½-inch plain or fluted tip

4 large egg whites, at room temperature

1 teaspoon cream of tartar

1 (18.9-ounce) box confetti cake mix

3 large egg whites, at room temperature

1¼ cups water

⅓ cup vegetable oil

Oil for deep-fat frying

Confectioners' sugar

Rainbow decorating sprinkles .

1. In a stand mixer, beat the egg whites on low speed until frothy. Add the cream of tartar and beat on high speed until stiff peaks form. In another bowl, mix the cake mix, egg whites, water, and oil until smooth. Carefully fold in the whipped egg whites until incorporated. Fill a large pastry bag with the batter and set aside to rest.

2. In a deep stockpot or deep fat fryer, heat the oil to 375°F. Line a baking sheet with paper towels.

3. Make the cakes. Cover the bottom of a pastry bag with your finger and ladle ½ cup of batter into the bag. Hold the pastry bag a couple of inches above the oil and carefully release your finger to distribute the batter, moving the pastry bag in a spiral motion to make the funnel cake.

4. Fry for 2 minutes on each side, or until golden brown, flipping with metal tongs or a frying spider. Set the cakes aside to drain on paper towels, and repeat with the remaining batter.

5. Dust the cakes with powdered sugar and garnish with more sprinkles. Serve warm immediately.

MAGICALLY NO-FAIL SUGAR COOKIES

These cookies are perfect for any occasion. Cut the cookies into
fun shapes like unicorns, moons, and stars. See "More Cookie Ideas"
on page 91 for more fun ideas with this versatile dough.

MAKES 18 cookies
PREP TIME 25 minutes
COOK TIME 20 minutes
YOU WILL NEED cookie cutters, piping bags fitted with ⅛-inch tips (if desired)

FOR THE COOKIES

2½ cups all-purpose flour

¼ teaspoon baking powder

¼ teaspoon fine salt

¾ cup granulated sugar

1½ sticks (¾ cup) unsalted
butter, softened

1 large egg, lightly beaten

1 teaspoon vanilla extract

FOR THE ROYAL ICING AND DECOR

3 large egg whites

1 teaspoon vanilla extract

4 cups powdered sugar

Food coloring (any colors
of your choice)

Sprinkles and decorating
sugar (optional)

TO MAKE THE COOKIES

1. In a small bowl, whisk together
the flour, baking powder, and salt
and set aside. In the bowl of a
stand mixer, beat the sugar and
butter until light and fluffy. With
the mixer on low, add the egg and
vanilla extract. Scrape down the
sides of the bowl and add the flour
mixture, mixing on low until just
combined.

continued »→

TO MAKE THE COOKIES (CONTINUED)

2. Turn the dough out and form it into a ball. Wrap in plastic wrap and chill for at least 20 minutes before baking.

3. Line two baking sheets with parchment paper or silicone baking sheets and preheat the oven to 350°F. On a clean, lightly floured surface, roll out the cookie dough into a large rectangle with about ¼-inch thickness. Cut into desired shapes, transfer to a baking sheet about 2 inches apart, and bake for 5–7 minutes or until the edges are lightly browned and set. Carefully transfer each cookie to a wire cooling rack and repeat with the remaining dough, making sure to gather any extra scraps left behind by the cutters.

TO MAKE THE ICING

4. In a large bowl of a stand mixer, combine the egg whites and vanilla and beat until frothy. Gradually add the powdered sugar and mix on low speed until the sugar is incorporated and the mixture is shiny. Increase the speed to high and beat until the mixture forms stiff, glossy peaks (about 5–7 minutes). Divide into bowls and stir in the food coloring, if desired. Transfer the icing to a pastry bag and pipe as desired. Decorate the cookies as you wish and let them set for at least 30 minutes.

UNICORN FOOD

MORE COOKIE IDEAS

Cookie Sticks

Once the dough is made, roll it out onto a clean, lightly floured surface into a large rectangle with about ¼-inch thickness. Cut into tall sticks about 4 inches high and ¾ inch wide. Transfer to a baking sheet about 2 inches apart and bake. Dip the cooled cookies about half the way into melted white chocolate candy disks and sprinkle with the desired decoration. To display, set the cookies upright in decorative cups.

Cookie Sandwiches

Fill 2½-inch circles of cookies with a 2-ounce scoop of vanilla ice cream, pressing to secure. Dip the sides in decorative sprinkles. Wrap in waxed paper and freeze for another hour before serving.

Supremely Simple Cookies

No time for icing? Roll the balls (about 2 tablespoons each) in a bowl of colored sugar. Transfer to baking sheets and press slightly to flatten. Bake as directed and let cool.

The Ultimate Sprinkle Guide

Whether you're topping a good old ice cream sundae or an over-the-top confectionary triumph, the sprinkle bar has been raised. The new wave of candy decor has the Internet going crazy over mixing a variety of textures, shapes, and sizes. See below for everything you need to know about sprinkle classification, plus ideas for mixes!

NONPAREILS

Nonpareils are tiny spheres that vary in size and color.

CONFETTI SPRINKLES

Think confetti, but in candy form! These sprinkles are round and flat and usually come in a variety of sizes.

JIMMIES

Jimmies are the most common variety of sprinkle; they are small and cylindrical.

DRAGÉES

Dragées are small metallic balls used for decorating (be warned; they are very crunchy!).

SANDING/CRYSTAL SUGAR

Sanding sugar is very fine colored sugar, and crystal sugar is much coarser. Both are dyed in a variety of colors.

EDIBLE GLITTER

Just like it sounds: glitter that is food-safe. Comes in a variety of color blends.

QUINS

Quins are confetti sprinkles cut into fun shapes: stars, hearts, and more.

RODS

Rods are the new sprinkle on the block. These sparkling cylinders are basically the bar version of a dragée.

EDIBLE PEARLS

Edible pearls are made of spherical sugar and are often larger than a standard dragée or nonpareil

There is no way to mess up a sprinkle mix! However you enjoy your color and texture combinations is up to you. Think about the treat you are trying to decorate and plan accordingly. For example, for a large cake, you need a lot of variety for complete coverage. Try lots of smaller nonpareils and pops of color with edible pearls. For smaller cupcakes, you can get funky with chunky metallic rods, different sizes of edible pearls, and a pinch of glitter.

These are a few of my favorite mixes, incorporating bold, contrasting colors and lots of fun shapes:

BIG & BRIGHT SKY MIX

1 part clear crystal sugar

+

2 parts royal blue nonpareils

+

1 part black nonpareils

+

1 part yellow edible pearls

+

1 part yellow star quins

+

a dash of gold disco glitter

PRETTY PINK UNICORN MIX

1 part pale pink nonpareils

+

1 part pale purple nonpareils

+

1 part purple jimmies

+

1 part white star quins

+

1 part light blue jimmies

+

a dash of silver disco glitter

DRINKS

The Unicorn Milkshake
The Real Deal Unicornachino
Champagne Candy Fizz
DIY Rainbow Sodas
Pink Lemonade Margaritas
White Hot Chocolate
Giggle Jelly Shots

THE UNICORN MILKSHAKE

We can all remember the great unicorn craze of 2017: the Unicorn Frappuccino. Sticky-sweet and filled with artificial mystery flavors, that treat made for a great photo, but could it be improved? Use natural fruits to dye your Unicorn milkshake, with no trip to the coffee shop required.

MAKES 2 milkshakes
PREP TIME 15 minutes
YOU WILL NEED 2 milkshake glasses

4 ounces white chocolate candy coating disks

1 tablespoon coconut oil

½ cup plus 2 tablespoons rainbow sprinkles

1 pint vanilla bean ice cream

1 cup chopped strawberries

½ cup fresh raspberries

1 cup milk of choice

Whipped cream

Toppings of your choice (see "Milkshake Toppers" on page 98)

1. In a microwave-safe bowl, melt the candy disks in the microwave in 30-second intervals, stirring in between, until smooth (about 90 seconds). Stir in the coconut oil and let cool slightly.

2. Make sure the glasses you are using are clean and very dry. Dip the lip of a cup into the melted chocolate, using a butter knife to spread the chocolate around the edges of the glass. Place the cups in the freezer for 2 minutes and then sprinkle with 2 tablespoons of sprinkles. Place the cups back into the freezer until the milkshake is ready.

3. In a blender, combine the ice cream, the remaining sprinkles, the strawberries and raspberries, and the milk, and blend until smooth and a pale pink color.

4. Pour the shake into the glasses and top with whipped cream and preferred toppings. Enjoy!

MILKSHAKE TOPPERS

Cotton candy

Rock candy sticks

Rainbow sour belt candy

Pocky sticks

Sprinkles or colored sugar

Rainbow swirl lollipops

Candy bark

Mini marshmallow

THE REAL DEAL UNICORNACHINO

See ya later, imitators—this unicorn drink *actually* has coffee in it! Make a classic white cappuccino at home, piled high with decadent whipped cream and extra sprinkles and glitter to make you feel fancy. You must use whole milk in this recipe: any low-fat version won't steam properly and won't be able to hold any toppings.

MAKES 2 cappuccinos
PREP TIME 15 minutes

½ cup espresso dark roast coffee, freshly ground*

1½ cups cold water

½ cup whole milk

4 ounces whipped cream

Sprinkles and edible glitter

*This recipe assumes that you don't have a cappuccino maker at home: if you're lucky enough to have one, substitute a shot of espresso for the called-for coffee in this recipe.

1. Place the ground coffee in the filter of a drip coffeemaker. Add water and brew to the maker's instructions.

2. Place the milk in a microwave-safe liquid measuring cup. Microwave on high for 1 minute, or until the milk is hot and forms bubbles around the edges.

3. Place a metal whisk into the cup and, as if you're trying to start a campfire, roll the whisk handle between your palms and rub it back and forth to create movement. If you have an electric frother, use it to whip the milk. Continue until at least a few inches of foam appears.

4. Divide the coffee evenly into two mugs and pour in the hot milk (reserving the foam). Carefully spoon the foam over the top of the coffee. Top with whipped cream and decorate with sprinkles and glitter.

CHAMPAGNE CANDY FIZZ

Glam up any boozy brunch with these sprinkle-tastic cocktails! A simple coating of white chocolate and a splashing of sprinkles is a perfect fit for any glitzy event. Top it off with your favorite sparkling rosé or champagne!

MAKES 4 drinks
PREP TIME 15 minutes
YOU WILL NEED 4 champagne glasses

4 ounces white chocolate candy coating disks

2 tablespoons mixed sprinkles of choice

4 ounces pomegranate juice

1 bottle sparkling rosé wine or other preferred sparkling wine

1. Wash and completely dry the champagne glasses. If any moisture remains, the chocolate will not adhere to the glass.

2. Place the disks in a microwave-safe bowl. Microwave in 30-second intervals, stirring after each interval, until the chocolate is smooth.

3. Lift a champagne glass and hold it horizontally over the bowl of melted chocolate. Using a butter knife, carefully spread a layer of melted chocolate on the top inch of the glass, gently twirling to remove any excess. Set the glass upright and let it sit for 2 minutes in the fridge (the chocolate will drip down the glass; this is okay). Repeat with the remaining glasses.

4. When the chocolate is still tacky but not completely wet, sprinkle the desired amount of sprinkles all around the glass. It's okay if a few sprinkles end up inside the glass. Let set in the fridge for 10 minutes.

5. Pour 1 ounce of pomegranate juice in each glass, top off with sparkling wine, and serve.

DIY RAINBOW SODAS

Italian sodas are one of my guilty pleasures—tangy, sweet fruit meets rich cream and comes together with a splash of bubbly fizz to make a perfect combo. Make a rainbow of sodas with store-bought flavors (see "The Spectrum of Syrup" below").

MAKES 2 sodas
PREP TIME 5 minutes

Ice cubes

4 tablespoons flavored coffee or soda syrups (such as Torani)

10 ounces club soda, chilled

2 tablespoons half and half (optional)

Whipped cream for topping (optional)

1. Fill tall highball glasses with ice. Pour 2 tablespoons of the syrup into each glass and top with club soda. Top off with 1 tablespoon of half and half in each glass.

2. Serve with whipped cream and stir with a straw to combine. Watch the colors swirl and enjoy!

THE SPECTRUM OF SYRUP

RED: cherry/cherry lime, strawberry, raspberry, grenadine

ORANGE: mango, tangerine, orange, passion fruit

YELLOW: pineapple, white peach, lemon

GREEN: kiwi, lime

BLUE: blue raspberry, blueberry

PURPLE: pomegranate, grape, red raspberry

PINK LEMONADE MARGARITAS

You've got the unicorn pool float; you just need a drink to match. This sweet and tart margarita is a perfect poolside sipper, complete with a glitter umbrella garnish.

MAKES 4 margaritas
PREP TIME 15 minutes
YOU WILL NEED 4 margarita glasses, paper cocktail umbrellas

FOR THE RIM

½ cup granulated sugar

1 tablespoon kosher salt

Zest of one lime

FOR THE DRINK

1 (12-ounce) can frozen pink lemonade (from concentrate)

2 cups frozen strawberries

4 cups water

2 cups tequila

2 cups ice

2 limes, wedged

1. In a small, shallow bowl combine the sugar, salt, and zest. Rub the zest into the sugar mixture with your fingers to distribute the flavor. Set the mixture aside until ready for use. Fill another shallow bowl with water and set aside.

2. In a blender, combine the frozen pink lemonade mix, strawberries, water, and tequila and blend until smooth, about 3 minutes. Add ice and blend another 2 minutes.

3. One glass at a time, turn the glasses over and dip about ⅛ inch of the rim into the water and then again into the sugar mixture. Fill the glasses with the margarita mix.

4. Garnish each drink with a lime wedge and paper cocktail umbrella.

WHITE HOT CHOCOLATE

Supremely decadent white hot chocolate is topped with marshmallows and whipped cream—it's enough sugar to put any unicorn over the rainbow! If you'd like to make this treat entirely from scratch, see page 81 for Glitter Pink Strawberry Marshmallows that would make beautiful toppers for this treat!

MAKES 2 servings
PREP TIME 12 minutes

4 cups milk of your choice

2 teaspoons vanilla extract

½ teaspoon kosher salt

8 ounces white chocolate chips

6 marshmallows, halved

Whipped cream

Disco glitter and sprinkles, for garnish

White chocolate biscotti, for serving

1. In a saucepan over medium-low heat, stir the milk, vanilla, salt, and chocolate chips and cook, stirring occasionally, until the chocolate is melted and the mixture comes to a soft simmer.

2. Remove from heat. Top with the marshmallows and whipped cream. Garnish with sprinkles if desired. Serve with biscotti or another preferred cookie for dipping.

GIGGLE JELLY SHOTS

Unicorns know how to party! Make these jelly treats adult-friendly by stirring in servings of vodka or another clear liquor of your choice. These treats take some time chilling in the fridge, so be sure to start this project the night before.

MAKES 30 (1-ounce) shots
PREP TIME 30 minutes
CHILL TIME 12 hours
YOU WILL NEED 30 disposable 1-ounce shot glasses

6 (3-ounce) boxes gelatin dessert mix (in rainbow colors)

6 cups boiling water

3 cups vodka

3 cups cold water

1. In a medium bowl, stir together one color of gelatin mix (starting with purple) and 1 cup of boiling water until the mix dissolves completely. Add ½ cup of vodka and ½ cup of cold water, stirring to combine.

2. Set shot glasses onto two rimmed baking sheets. Pour 1 tablespoon gelatin mix into each cup and let chill for 1 hour.

3. Repeat with the remaining colors, layering from purple to red in rainbow order.

4. It's party time!

HOW TO MAKE
DAZZLING ICE CUBES

If there's one way to make your drink stand out, it's by using show-stopping ice cubes! These cubes get their color from fresh fruit slices and fresh herbs, melting into gorgeous garnishes for your drinks and cocktails. If you want more color, add pureed fruit or fruit juice to each cube. As they melt, the fruit will subtly flavor the drink as well as make it beautiful.

Fill an ice cube tray with a variety of the fruit filling choices below. For superclear cubes, bring a pot of water to boil and let it cool to room temperature. If you don't mind cloudy cubes, just use tap water and fill the trays with it, leaving some room for the cubes to expand. Keep in mind that the fruit will float to the top. Freeze for at least four hours or until frozen solid.

RED ICE	ORANGE ICE	YELLOW ICE	GREEN ICE	BLUE/PURPLE ICE
Strawberry slices	Peach slices	Lemon slices	Cucumber slices	Edible pansies
Pomegranate arils	Cubed mango	Pineapple chunks	Kiwi slices	Black plum slices
Fresh raspberries	Edible marigold flowers		Fresh herbs such as basil or mint	Blueberries
			Green grapes	

INDEX

RACHEL JOHNSON is a food writer/stylist and enthusiastic
Instagrammer who believes in Stupid Good Food. She creates
recipes that are easy to follow and inspire fun in the kitchen.
Her past work includes *Chowhound*, *Cooking Light Magazine*,
Bon Appetit, and *Edible Austin*, among others. She enjoys
pizza, feminism, and creating joy through food. Rachel lives
in Austin, TX with her pups and full pantry.

 @stupidgoodrachel

 @stupidgoodfood